The Clockwork Gift

Also by Claire Crowther:

Stretch of Closures

CLAIRE CROWTHER

The Clockwork Gift

Shearsman Books
Exeter

First published in the United Kingdom in 2009 by
Shearsman Books Ltd
58 Velwell Road
Exeter EX4 4LD

www.shearsman.com

ISBN   978-1-84861-032-3

for my grandchildren

CONTENTS

I

THE HEREBEFORE

PETRA GENETRIX

for Selima Hill

I won't replace lost wedding cutlery,
its broad straight limbs,
with new shallow spoons,
their writhing shoulderless handles—

Lines get broken.
All I see in museums
is the frozen watchfulness of a previous home.
Ancient knives found under Eden Walk are flints

polished in an age defined by how it ate.
There's no matching greenstone and dolomite
though I could still buy old patterns,
shell, feather, rat tail.

'Granny, did you throw away your silver?'
'The table of the moon is laid with it.'

LIVE GRENADE IN SACK OF POTATOES STORY

The schizoid boy who never takes his pills
and has been ordered not to visit any female
family member, here he comes, half-naked,
down to my basement. Later, a police dog bites
his scrotum. I buy chips and biscuits. Mutter
names. I take care of these grandchildren.
Like that unfed, sleepless child – the number
of games I thought up, but she's live, a grenade,
buried and ready to explode, dug up
decades after the war, lost in a sack
of potatoes. They come for my expertise.
It's worth their battering the door
to share my anger. *Nonna, oma, nain.*

ONCE TROUBLESOME

*'Let them call her a wicked old woman! she knew she was
no such thing.' Vita Sackville-West, All Passion Spent*

It isn't New Year yet so Happy *What*?
Till then, it's Boxing Day every morning.
Empty bags hang off the radiators.
Chilly: hot
        cold
                Cordelia position.
           Did it mean
we didn't love each other
that morning he gave me up
though that same night he said let's marry?
        My striped dress hung
             along my body
            bounced
           boldened
         bitmapped
my abdomen as I walked, a balloon
           sinking back down
          its own string
      after the decision.
The baby would have had to sleep in a drawer.
            Immortalists
(not you who refuse to believe improbable notions)
think:
       the smallest cell refuses to die
       in its everness.
Now I live in an attic
garden is the chewed melon skin of sky.
Old bins, old books. Death's hardly ethical
in the light of such continuity. Last week,
the CEO of a charity named in my will
wrote to suggest ways to retrieve what I've lost.

Look, Christmas photos
        of others' other
            children. After
                    Pocoyo, Juggling Balls.

OPEN PLAN

They took the walls away without warning.
The roof floated, a miraculous *over* of shelter.
We were caught out. We cooled quickly. A sty?

My hands made paws? My lover stamped in the open.
Who took the decision? Editorials argued
about iconoclasm. We'd had a tradition

of opening the inside but obscuring doors.
But doorlessness isn't just trailing ivy
over a letterbox or bricking the front

to look like the side. Our family walls were all sides.
The trick was to show passers-by a gleam of room.
One of our walls had had an exquisite *trompe l'oeil*

library. No stranger could find a way in
and no one knew how we had done it, which book
the idea came from. Every unwalled home

can't be called a ruin. I missed the rally.
Thousands met in a park—that seems so ironic.
Were they protesting about their gazebos?

My bed is a perfect copy of straw, comfortable.
I hold you as close as when we were walled in,
though nearer the pavement, though clearer to them.

MINE, THEN

for those grandmothers who parent AIDS orphans

We sat on the bench outside the clinic
and I explained that they might need medicine.

I said, 'There is weather coming,
full of variety.

Wouldn't you like an umbrella
if it rains?' On the way home

it was as easy to make them laugh
as to find a vein.

I could see straight through that mousey light
to evening,

past houses pale
as my own finger,

across the pewter surface of salted road
edged by leafless trees.

The ground heaved
with sealed-in bluebells.

They worried I would be less upset
than when my own child died.

You need one person to be loved by
like a lightning flash needs dousing in a peach cloud.

Xylotheque

My husband mocks the ghost who hovers near me
on walks. A ghost wouldn't climb a stile
or skirt cows so widely. And why would she edge
round barely flooded fields? Leaky shoes?

Aren't ghosts violent, my husband suggests.
No, you need a body for that, to be
as well as mean and seem, though the ghost wears
blue jeans, sequinned boots and says

she was bullied for being beautiful
as a teenager and loved a mechanic
from Dollis Hill at twenty. The ghost noticed me
in the doctor's surgery. I held

a child who snuffled my hand like an animal.
Dying is being born. You imprint on the person
you see last. I remember her panic.
Receptionists corralled the waiting room.

Calling her up now seems like human-stealing.
My husband mocks: 'You saw a death. Why
exaggerate?' Maybe because, without ghosts,
we are a wooden library, books about wood

bound in wood with leaves for pages, words,
the seeds and nuts of ancient beech, birch, oak
and rowan. I look for her where
box trees curl like knots of neglected hair.

ARCHAEOLOGY

We used the big spade or the fork with long tines and played
on soft ground
on wet days

planting old packets, seeds, back of the drawer, labelled
God's Blue,
black

full stops that peppered Grandmother's box as we levered it
out of the puddle
we'd dug.

The cardboard dissolved fast, we wanted her out. (She *wasn't* dead.)
We melted
the tearing

stuff from her surfaces till she lay peeled, brown as the wet
clay
and corners

of mouth, eyes, tightened in an imagined smile
at the terrible
rule:

first to run from the body must go back and bury the bits
of knicker
and bead.

Mrs Campbell of Ballimore

'(Sir Henry Raeburn) was often more successful with the
portraits of middle-aged or elderly women of pronounced
character than he was with those of young and very pretty
girls.'
        Exhibit note, National Gallery of Scotland, Edinburgh

Take note of my grandmother's white veil
over grey curls—
                despite grey cloth
gloving her right hand
and a forefinger pointing down—

because look, how more nets close
her neck in white—
                though her dress is blackened
by a cloak.

Whether you acknowledge
that sunset waters its last light over her face
or observe the topmost branches are darkening
with oil, still, her red cheeks plump
all wrinkles out.

                I stole her blood
and now he haunts her with me, hunting it.

WOMAN, PROBABLY ONE OF THE FATES

*'This is one of a number of representations of hideously ugly old
women by the same hand . . .'*
       Exhibit note, National Gallery of Scotland, Edinburgh

When wrinkles etch so deeply they lattice neck
and muzzle forehead, skin takes over,

makes a fabric of old stone. What I see
in my inner arm when it's bare and bent, raising a glass,

is Fate holding her drapery. It's what I expect
though bones would be more likely. Here is an outstanding
           breastbone.

And veins tunnel out the hand. While marble grabs its opportunity
to empty sockets of eyes and teeth – skin is resistance.

EMPIRE

It was all Latin to us
     the way the box hedge
          tore through a white dress
of *convolvulus arvensis.*
Buxus sempervivens.
     We looked the lot up
          in a coffee table book
Familiar Wild Flowers.
Toad flax and poppy
     went for a strategy
          of abundance that year
we moved in
but only watercoloured
     the tough old box.
          The successful cohabitees,
in the end, were drab,
dressed with London cool.
     Ajuga reptans,
          named by Pliny
for its power to drive away
who knows what,
     cowered, bore
          only seven or eight
flowers to the head.
Other labiates,
     dead-nettle and betony
          and the supposedly graceful
Festucca elatior,
cramped under wicker fingers
     that could slit hands,
          your eyes once.
You tried to dig it out.
Its roots are infected

by some virus
            that turns the clay soil
round the stems to cement.
The tiny eyes of its leaves
      flash open each year
            among dog grass,
dog campion, dog roses.

Experience

The woman let off Death Row walked through a gorge
of chaotic limestone left by meltwater
and saw men everywhere.

They were climbing the steep and overhung sides.
Their feet flexed in thin shoes, toeing
crevice after crevice.

Their hands pried the split crag for brokenness.
They hung
and carefully worked out each nodule of rock

rejecting the frailty of this or that stone,
clicking in the knot
that would hold them from falling back to the passage.

She ignored arrows, made her own path
through tall-stalked, small-headed ferns and young ash,
past a feral goat, newish horns knuckling up,

across cinquefoil-buttered grass, near-invisible swellings
of bluebell seed, a memory of leaving home—
or maybe a promise.

The climbers weren't enjoying the view.
They climbed for the sake of the stone. One stopped
in a patch of sun, refusing to carry on

trusting the handshake of rock and rope
though below each man another looked up
holding a thin string.

She was looking for innocence
like an older woman standing over her young husband
allowing an undoing of long hair.

The Blood Queen

Here Two Ladies Sat To See The View
Every Day. They made as much of it as if they were the ones
murdering the plough in a field as rich with stones as currant cake.

They saw the understorey of King's Wood:
holly, spindle, whitebeam, hazel, dogwood, coppiced ash, field
  maple.
Woodpeckers nested in resurrected wych elms.

And once in sixty years, one saw the dragon
of Wurminster Sleight, flaming from Dinder to Dulcote, slithering
  through Herb Paris.
Maleficence, bare-armed as sun, rose up and stood

over the Tor, swinging a long wind
round his head. It was fierce on that north side. Below, a coin of
  silver silk was sewn
in the Abbey green and other fields slipped

under water, seeing the wyvern. The woman went further
than sight, into a valley where woods were at war, bluebell falling
  to wild garlic. Drifts of
dead fern cloaked the lake. Deep

hoof marks clove mud, red as live muscle
sliced up and laid at her feet. Scree had fallen as far as it could.
Midair, trees had frozen, longhaired with moss.

A river would have unified things
but dry stones lining the gorge were crazy for human feet. At
  Gurney Slade, the seat held
June asleep while Ivy, fast as a grass snake,

wormlike, not glistening but damp-skinned,
ran down steps made by tree-roots neatly observing the regular
        fall of height as
each ridge stretched across a manmade path.

The dragon rested in a ruin off Grunter's Lane,
fenced in with wind-clicked metal. Dreaming of a hidden well,
        June cursed: *May*
eyes that fly with Maleficence, fly once.

May the bent pin of my curse cut water so deeply
its surface can't heal. Who will watch the whitehaired moon with me?
        Ivy, dead in
freedom soared, hatching its shadow with tiny bones.

THE THIKE

Here in Hob's Moat we know
a thike is not a species of devil
but, unhappily, receives attention.

A mammal, the small-lifed thike,
flourishes in our dry moat
among those buried outside graveyards.

Ranked first of unknown fauna,
a thike is easily seen from the A road,
fooling near its wood. The number of thikes

casually shot is high.
Celebrities on Channel Five News
have endorsed the policing of thike-baiters.

The community is stunned. The prevalence
of a unique English animal
is like a local murder. A primary teacher,

our most famous resident, author
of ninety books, has lectured to us often.
He says we have been thinking like Australians.

Ask instead what factors influence
the occurrence of a moated society.
No doubt our thikes begin to feel extinct.

But the mood of Hob's Moatians is hopeful
while ThikeSafe Company men,
wearing white, squat on concrete in garages,

open plastic lunch boxes and release
the thikes they have secured with nothing more
than broken clothes hangers. Remember,

when you hear a Fastruk lorry
reverse, screeching, thikes lack ears.
We elect the animals we harbour.

THE WILD LIFE OF GOODBYE

I worked out how thikes talked, by touch.
They combed that butter-coloured fur with a long revv up
each strand, measuring distance from the head, pulling or pushing.

> They gave each other permission to
> touch—the neck, underbelly—and spoke
> fast. Linguists charted their range of
> sounds; semantics, no.

I learned to hear them say, *Come back to the hollow.*
Heard their names. I have no idea, being a poet,
whether they lived in peace or in violence like their end.

> That older female by the traffic island,
> hair flattened—how the rush hour traffic
> rubber-necked to see her, a thike out of
> her moat. That mass of blackening yellow
> on the *News*.

The cullers left the feet alone. Thike feet
stick to any surface, their soles a suction-pad
beneath boneless muscle. The carcasses
smell of fresh grouting.

It was hot but I didn't notice how short of breath
the sky, how a summer lung can't speak
without breaking. From my eyrie above
the *Medieval Fayre*, no homogeny to hair,
hair holds no hegemony for crowns.

> Everyone is feral, a deer counts notes,
> a dog tugs a child's paw with hands like
> teeth. In Hob's Moat today, an ill pale yolk

of sun. Pheasants dashed into the wood.
The male watched the female dip her head
in steaming clay.

The grass! It's lost its tread. Cruising thunder makes breeze
panic. Against the window, my arms are strips of silver,
run moon solder.

Sleeping on a Trampoline

I find her sleeping on our large tramp,
neatly in the middle. Heels on the metal
springs. A human thike.

A child buzzes in my head, trapped.
Usually a child takes my hand and up, whee,
a few minutes, then brings me down, my feet

plunge into sturdy skin, the palm throws me
back at a long day's sky like a duck, shuttlecock,
bee, the smack of body against my bones,

not-hug, not-massage, not-relax-you're-cared-for,
only a continent moving by my right shoulder.
Breathing, not jumping: I watch her till she wakes,

the human thike. Silent, though this one talks
for hours. 'When I was born, I was so desperate
to get out, I called to a passing neighbour,

from the uterus. She told my mother
I was about to jump. You never hear the word
outside Surrey. You're thikey, not a woman,

not a man. A night timer. There's always
someone who saw the thike in the woods at night
or sitting in the square at three a.m.

You never ask, what were *you* doing
out, spying on the thike in the small hours.
There isn't any therapy for thikes,

only for hate crimes. Other villages
make saints, celebrities. Ours makes thikes.
I don't have to accept this? And you're a woman?'

It's not because I'm dirty
It's not because I'm clean
It's not because I kissed a thike
inside a space machine

It was a common word once. Pepys' diary,
earliest known mention, bar mummers' plays:
Home where the thike is come out of the country.

Keats' letter: *I think upon crutches like the thikes*
in your Pump Room. Matthew Arnold, a rare
attempt at definition: *Thikes were boys*

whose good character was easily regressed.
Monk Lewis: *She wasn't conversational. Whether shy*
or as a result of her theikism, no one could tell.

I ask what I should call her. 'Say hello
fartface, for all I care.' Our new estate
is carefully designed not to be repetitive.

That's why we moved back to the village from town.
(Not strangers. Remember the summerhouse factory?
We've got a memento, the old sign: SOUND

YOUR HOOTER at 5 MPH.) Paint flakes off the words.
Some large houses, some small, irregular roofs,
red, green, grey tiles, a pond to fulfil

the quality of life clause. Nobody said
there were still thikes. Grasshopper baby,
she's shivering. I can tuck her in again,

cover her with spit. Or jump till dawn.
Bouncing is resisting repetition, not
enduring it. My feet slip on news

paper covering the tramp, layers starting
to compost, a thick cold grey pudding, marble-ised
with black streaks. A black rim lines each frame

of sky as if glass draws away from wood.
Whee. Up a string of path, spun from the machine
of height to its overhang, its large mouth.

I reach my hand into sorbet, crystalline height,
whipped up business. She is only a crescent moon
of shoulder. The village job that nobody does.

We lean into the machine. The magnifying
glass of dark shows me what I've missed,
pushes past my artefacts, leaving them heaving.

Gradual grey smears round clouds and fists
of treetops. A hiccough of birds. Like going up
to bed, stairs set into the wall,

a chimney into rock, so steep. It's a mistake
to come back down again. You'll be damaged
by blacked out windows, masked eyes, silence,

locked doors. It makes you agree to wrong
ideas even at slow speeds unless
someone warns you first, sounding the hooter.

THE VIRGINITY OF DECAY

Hooped in my own arms, I lie and hope
that I'll like flying soon. The off, steep up:

> I hate them now. The slippery stile of height
> as if mounting a sword-leaved thistle, as if
> runners, spindles and nodes of iron poked
> through a railing as broken as trees below
> dragging their ruined canopies. The stones
> stick out anyhow.

And then the climb down anxious ground to see

> a colony of Lesser Horseshoe bats in
> derelict Lime Kiln Cottage. To find only
> blurry pictures fixed to a lock, their smell a
> smokey ghost at Slocker's Hole where ash
> thighs grip

a block of limestone and abandoned engines melt.

SUMMERHOUSE

It stalked me in its brochures, Majestic, Alpine.
At last I found the factory, grown-over
down a lane. Nobody there? A fifties'
sign in the forecourt: *Sound Your Hooter*.

There was a sediment of geranium pots
on the balcony of the showhouse.
I talked to the manager in purest Wilton,
which he'd used to carpet Rome.

But I could see the future: torn wallpaper,
swathes of web, buckled boards, damp,
and under a raddled Cedar Red porch,
the visits and revisits of a vixen.

Shaman Mam-Gu

It is a shadowy night-like light today; car after car,
shiny but sepia. But look at us!
We aren't hueless! Tiny pedestrians scampering
in between lorries, white wisps of a granddaughter's hair
against my hennaed Afro, her blanched hand clasping
my red-nailed thumb. The sounds are of day—ambulance whining
down a No Entry with full spectrum Doppler effect while nose
after nose of plane parts the cloudbank, ready for Heathrow.

And our actions have been anything but pallid: an old woman
        scolding
the police who held a child. Her arms flicker. An officer
turns the flat of his hands toward her, berating air.
Between grey-hooded girl and red hair, our staring
is so healthy it could cure break-bone fever.
Lorries at an amber light talk in gravelly voices,
unbrick, rebrick this dark afternoon.

HOARD

In the garage all day, bringing together kept bits,
wheel, leg, strip of metal, unrolled yard of fabric.

She had believed she'd make something of what was in here:
artificial intelligence or art

but has made nothing when he comes home
only thought about how the dust has settled

on flowers that once sang *Lillibullero*. Maybe
there wasn't enough light from one bulb, though unshaded

or it was too cold to take a scatter of things onto the patio
where, anyway, suds of many baths float from jammed drains.

ROOM UNDER THE STAIRS
for Anne-Marie Fyfe

Crushed against stair rises, no
    pushing the hard margins apart
        but I tried to lounge, one foot
            buried in a flank of brushed cotton,

a lost bale. Outside, on the stairs,
    my mother's feet, stubby substitutes
        for words. My grandmother's steps
            breathed in-out-in to the top.

Dark books hunched like handles
    of cases in the nearly midnight
        in there. Every folded muscle
            ached. Upside bones were crazed

with needles. Air, packed with scales
    from unfinished wall, struggled into my lungs.
        I was filling two tins and closing
            smiling dog lids when my mother slid

across red tiles into the light rule
    around the door. We went shopping.
        Who can say
            why I had to collapse my imagination?

THE HEREBEFORE

The grandmother sings to the marvellous stove
and the child draws another inscrutable house.
                                    Elizabeth Bishop

It's indefensible, falling in love with the dead,
but every so often a young woman, hungry
and broke, brakes a borrowed car, leans forward,
listens to the bard in the marketplace

and sees the black and white of what hasn't happened
to her yet: a grey basket of bread
turning brown. Similarly, an old woman
in black among men wearing white, apron and shirt,

watches to see their future in what's been stopped.
Of the unrealised celebrities on the cobbles,
one is lulled by the absence of home into speaking
to me: *Stare into my memory.* Sleep being sideways,

we sidle into clay, set and stamped down
by poets, ice shaving soft hairs from our skin.
The newly dead can hear for half an hour;
what can the old, dead for a century, hear?

Who she is, a granddaughter knows, myself:
unexpected as a voile caul of rain
on the oak or the minute pools that hang in bracken
to look through. *Sun, you're not the only thing*

that thinks it's the centre, raced round by worlds.
My herebefore, I'm no less your granddaughter
than one who would stay down a lane narrow enough
to need indents to let another pass,

who would have liked you to wait and see if the work
of eternity rolled up. But you ran off
where pink blackberry flowers net dark-leaved
old nettles and humble the water lilies.

In no-man's land meet me, set a time:
the lattermath of war. There I rock on the steel,
slit to ribbons above powered pleats of water
falling weeded from the mirage of a still pool

to its spun slip of lace torn off by black ground.
Two bridges cross the same moat, allowing travellers
to stay separate. A heron looks up: someone
has ground a stone against wet grass. Then he ducks

again and his neck coils into black and white
before straightening, rising slowly, the long
bottle-stopper beak pointing west
as the lost woman arrives, her lover lifting

an empty crash of raw silk, a gorgeous
light mass but she is aged by the sun
far into rut and root. No one would know her.
None of us know her logic of flight

to that old village function in a long dress,
children in imitation paging behind her,
a train of family holding the fabric of future
carefully out of the mud. Wedding in memoriam.

She ran over fields, jumping stiles, into woods,
disappearing, a rabbit, flapping her handmade jacket

pockets. Coming back isn't what the dead do.
You lied when you said you were always home for tea.

Stay still, lean on your hand-cut stick, thorn
or new ash picked from a growing hedge or from wild
seeded trees, young, straight, unbarked
except for thin grey skin. Trees throw a thousand

buds out of fingertips that point to our ancient
cutting, thronged with stranded sticks of sapling.
The thinnest trees have tried to seed, grown
a bit, been defeated. *The gullies, the pores in the grass*

filled with dead plants—it's how we breathe.
Mind is here, thinking through its litter.
The bike man, mending her Princess Sovereign,
lugged and brazed, with gold-lined mudguards,

ding dong bell, tyre-driven dynamo headlamp,
skirt guards and wicker basket, says: 'Every cell
has been replaced in my shop. None of it is truly
her machine.' I drive to Hob's Moat

where there are no weathercocks, buy red silk
with blue stripes, anything rather than walk
the fields in their rotational rest. She waits,
her shoes battered as oak bark. Rather than find

no thorn and nothing branched,
tethered, only the suicide-flower, ragwort
winched by a chlorophyll cord. We are braked
not scotched. 'Has she dropped off the earth?'

My grandfather sent a card explaining. So why
do I find her watching an arts festival
in the square when a future for my crossroad
and estate is all I am looking for?

If I've misrepresented her, a grandmother
painted beside a candle who claims gas light,
it's because rain diffuses our images.
She would have been in her element, arc-lit

in gold water, being filmed on stage
reading poems about sun, flanked by flowers,
her face a gleam of all her profiles projected
at once. We would watch her cross the wall

with her words, the woman below copying
the woman above, an image of synchronicity,
as tightly turned as her every stall at my desk.
No skull but a new-coined queen.

II

St Anne's Apocrypha

THIRTEEN

One hand holding a board, the two-foot man
balances.

Standing on his head, handed a can of beer,
drinks.

Towered over by fish-net tights and high wire,
juggles.

Flaming through hoops, spinning a lariat,
tethers

girls. Does what the tall men do. My grandson
grips

a can, his ticket to Spurs, a mobile. Mouth
open.

Unexpected Goal

A thin fall of similarity misted allotments blending
into the white ribbon of car park stretched out to dry
beside a station kicking trains through to other cities.

The brush factory leaned on the high street. A colonnade
of young trees dithered, snappy at the bole. Multichimneyed
mansions and flattened chimneyless estates looked to noon

for dazzle. Hard not to be disappointed. No lightning rip
into even one dead brain cell to resurrect
a clear image. Only the usual promise to clarify

while, instead, flags hung out of windows—St George
overlooking a grey-haired woman striker playing
with a boy among bikes left where they fell, mid-roar.

STREET FOOTBALL

You could hear new tines of glass, let out like children,
stick the wind. Then the Shrove ball flew above

the greensand caves, yells drumming it north past
the Brewery and the Dust Destructor. It landed on

a drunk, shaking a collecting tin. Back from alleys,
yards and windows, up, up until it staggered

toward Turner, Sauberge—where my mended kettle
was ready on Ash Wednesday—the ball bounced off

the diapers of Chitty's brickwork, sprinkled Nanny Puttock
from her fountain—come in, boys, she beckoned—soared

as far as Pump Corner, brushed black suits hung
along Fielders' window. Tall Percy palmed the last

drop of rain. Because my hands had practised taking
Matchpeller's dog when it sprang, my bones were fit to break

to confiscate the ball and—flash—no-one stopped
a grandmother catch, a game finish. Men boiled over

Master Woodger's muffins. Fattened, Taffer Boult,
dressed as Grandma Wolf, stood up on gouty feet.

THE CLOCKWORK GIFT

Behind the glass in Burgerzoo, fingers probed
bark. Elongated aye-aye fingers.
Larvae hid in hollows.

A tape of crickets over Blur. My granddaughter
opened a Kid's Bag. I wound
the clockwork gift.

Her legs were striped with shades of pink wool.
When did I think
of wearing black and grey?

She'd been dispensed by her mother with rose
skirt, coat. The aye-aye was tethered
to a tree trunk by its tail

twice body length. 'What's an omen of evil?
Why can't an aye-aye go home?'
A naked ear turned right, left.

ST ANNE'S APOCRYPHA

i *Joachim Emeritus*

Here's what Joachim wanted
her to find: a bent black gas tap, unused
for years, on a ledge beside the door. An old plastic watering can,
nozzle arched and long as the stem of a flower. No plants.

A twenty-one inch screen presenting
a document titled *The Wrong Sort of Electricity*.
Awards laid, stacked or propped in frames.
A blackboard: a set of five points, _The World Watching_ underlined,
a heading OLD TABLE. One window blinded,

the other open to a view of roof tops.
The phone slipping off the end of the desk, its wire dangling
into a half-open drawer. Lever Arch files labelled
Strain Balance.

ii St Anne's Hard Hat

Maria put down her Dyson in the doorway. 'Enough
of this. You'll sack me if you get pregnant and by the way

you're only fifty-three. Here, put this on, it's cool.'
The scarf she handed her employer spread, a cloth

of morning glory; blackberry bramble. It covered the long
garden where Ornamental Crab, John Downie, fruited

red, yellow, along the post. Green dust had coated her
since morning. 'And put this on.' The new hard hat.

Anne strimmed along the chine. Finger bones of root
shook free from soil. 'Inside, I feel twenty

but what can I look at and not feel barren?
Even these bitter apples have come to good.'

iii *Joachim's Escape*

The Astroturf was powdered with the dust of physicists
who measure, under the Jura,

the half-life of elementary particles. 'Come on, Dark Matter.'
Joachim, their captain, used his head—

'*thck*. Where are you, Exiles?' Thirty years since cold chambers
of liquid hydrogen warmed up

yet on came the Bubble Chamber teams, red-shirted Kaons and
        Pions,
still chasing protons

the millisecond before it boiled, smacking electrons into negative
        action,
recording the infinitesimal lives of goals.

iv Honeymoon Outside the Golden Gate

The language was immaculate.
Joachim chatted to the driver: 'Bernex was a village then,

the prettiest. I would cycle right into CERN.'
White horses, like tall sheep, raced in their hundreds.

A plane hung on its vertical vapour trail above a chateau
with four square turrets and many ruined barns.

It was a revisitation in old age
of what had become angels, clouds of cherubim heads.

v *St Anne's Epigraph*

while the sun instilled the night
in their window,
black glass
from a radiant, dangerous furnace,

and geese raced left to right like words,
each bird whirring
in its letter,
rewriting a written sentence:

Come back, day, un-
broken.
Come
back day, unbroken.

vi Mary's Bargain

Mary, in Anne's spare room, huddled
under a hand-embroidered throw found
in a sale, crumpled beyond its physiology.

It cost pence due to the odd maths
of reduction – Fifty Percent! of the sale price,
which was Fifty Percent!! of the first Price Cut

plus An Extra Ten Percent Today!!!
She owned not one thing Anne would call exquisite.
Casual stable keeper, Mary even calls her body art.

vii Anne's Bequest

A purifier turned, this way, that way,
filtering old air for dust like words or specks like sounds.
There weren't too many books for its task.

The pages fluttered when she turned them to it.
Mary breathed calmly, once the particulates
of unnaturally pressed sense were combed for thought.

viii *Grandmother of God*

At six centimetres dilated, the acupuncturist asked Mary to bear the wriggle of hair-pin in her wrist. In a corner, a tap was dripping. A woman shivered loudly, contracting inside her curtains. A giant fish swung a fin in the exposed roof of the new atrium. A folded pink strait-jacket was archived in a glass case.

Ordinary bodies were painted as cloisters. Anne's bones ached for SUNLIGHT: the word was machine-embroidered on the cotton sheet, and sheet and bed were each named ANNIVERSARY. She waited among the hospital artworks, purple leaves, cut beaten metal waterfalls, haggling with memories of how she had done it.

ix St Anne's House

Her ex-chapel on Head Hill walled
its rooms with curtains. If a visitor laughed,
the whole house heard, as in chapel days.
The confidence of house-names – *St Anne!*

x Visitation

The Levels lay exhausted after a licking
from low cloud. The rhynes overflowed
toward a Mendip boundary exacted from mud.
'Granny, it's me. It's been a shit year.'

Her grandson was having trouble with conversion:
leaving home, teaching the toughest kids.
They planned his gap year on a balcony
at stained-glass level. She remembered the anchoress

who escaped, brought back like a slashed shoe
to be hidden in thatch, and her own gran, a window
welcoming endless souls. Fearful stock he came from,
heath-women with steel deer legs in bramble country.
.

Outside the Beauty School

Twilight Hour for Senior Customers.
The trees turn, in a May
that pulls their branches gently inside out,
and paints charcoal bark with green polish.

While trees think they're not trunk-stopped
on one spot, it is as good a season as any
for wings to pulse, swollen reddish-pink;
for a heart to rise to it, float up and beat in the wind.

Turn and Out of It

As summer ice must dance when a thaw re-orders the season,
I cool myself this November.

Assembled layer on layer over late months of summer,
the fire is ready to fuse.
Only the toughest sticks are still green,
the rest brittle brown disposable by rubbing, eyes
after sleep, nightmares into dust.

> Breaking up a light—pulsing it, beading
> it—is one way to interpret the dark. I
> helter-skelter between dots, dashes,
> nail-heads, eye-whites

but here the flames candle something naked to see with,
that looks through the schwa-soft wind.

KEY STAGE
for Bessie, who suffered from dementia

In a shop
where keys are copied,
my daughter asks for her own.

The boy takes mine.
His overalls are oily from the machine.
We wait.

She reminds me: 'You must carry it
always, it locks you out
as well as lets you in. If it sticks

to begin with, don't panic.'
It wears smooth in time.
She has gone

out for years without me.
Now she will come home alone with my key,
enter my emptiness as an adult,

bar out the night
whose shine
is from dead stars,

and accept what she sees of me
through doors
she has opened.

BACKPACKER

She steps over frogs defended with poison
in the forest of Bastimentos.
Asleep above her, a sloth suddenly drops

onto orchids. She walks the waterfall.
After her ride over a necklace of islands,
whoa: the boatman holds her horse,

speaks guari guari to calm him.
Rice sack sails nose past other retirees
in Parque Simon Bolivar. She's not with them

eating Johnny cakes but, rare as an egg
laid by a leatherback turtle, she smiles
through the bars of a waterfront jail in Bocas.

Ubi Sunt

Where are they now, the transparent walkways,
office to office, tear-shaped desks,
the turning necks of chairs, head rests?

Sand blows through the levels. At night,
the corners are penetrated with floodlight.
The high cheekbones of the Place de Dome,

the Comfort Hotel, glint. Bodies move
like smoke on granite mirrors. Not my storey:
that's empty, panes broken, its eery

insides deny I ever started there,
young, skipping up the run of stair;
deny I worked my whole life behind glass.

SOLAR SCIENTIST

A naked blonde lies, parallel to our window,

> huge across an ad. Her heels, legs, reflect
> on our pillows. We can't rush by like cars
> but, spattered with her, Keith clings to his
> journal. Tomorrow, a tube will push past
> his prostate, applying fibre-optics

as does the skin of this electric picture

> worn so little compared to our lignite
> whose fuel can't fire us up again, and like
> his own experiment to flow through fibre
> veins

the wild material that flashes, stuns,

stark as an ambulance, the sun.

AGE REFUSES A GRANDDAUGHTER

Nobody can see in;
I'm a tower woman.
What a combination of shadows and angles of light.
I wave, I must open the window,
lean out to the perilous.
Down there, each machine is allowed its sound.
I hear my father siren, chatter, groan,
guttural trucks.
My turret captures girls with long hair
and longings to be locked up in
or just up in,
small, concentrations of years.

My house swings as it steps,
Baba Yaga's house
revved up on barley sugar.
The background day is black.
Your eyes are like mercury.
I can't have you.
You're not my child.
Big problem, your narrative.
It drags against my dream
so vivid, raw oat curls
off the flapjack. You'll come
to see for yourself one day,
flesh stalk,
stump relation.

You'll go to see my grannies.
There they sit, full of tea, as young as you.
Don't you ignore me like they do.
You're no herebefore, you're the hereafter.

Turret room, it's not easy to make it cosy,
its back against the wall of a tower house.
A playground swing. It swirls its iron round
your head. Dangerous rocking.

Abuelita

Praise to the grandmother high on a balcony.
Its wearied fencing shuts space into miles.
She scrubs a coconut shell.
Pours dirty water over a herb pot.
Dust from black deposits under her feet blow
towards a terracotta emperor astride
a vent rattling out hot air.
She varnishes her hundredth soap dish
while seven floors below, white van roofs
lie like water lilies and glittering gems
of cars are packed with crystalline couples.

I praise the turret she hangs on.
Gardenless, it humbles the low villas,
the opal-crusted scarab beetles on wheels.

Dusk in a Royal Park

To move from here, trees have twisted in flinches
till they hollowed and the wind swept through,
scouring dryads out, the resistant life
in the copses, spinneys, coppices all the same:
under their canopies and crowns, a labour of burls.

I'm treading deciduous water,
sliding on shiny scales of evergreen leaves
and moved by profoundly dried wrecks
of tree root and thickened boles,
the tension wood of ancient oak,
dull kaleidoscope of rind girdled with rings
cut to slow growth or kill
their life-long effort to move,

however slowly. A white dog carelessly prowls,
head down among the fallen,
gaunt, delimbed oaks. But since last year,
one decapitated log has slithered up
hillock and hummock against the grain of grass.

If a log can approach me,
stared at by parakeets and deer,
then you could have. But it's the cull
when every gate is locked at midnight.

FATALITY

The car mechanic mentions worn linkage,

that changes in the arm make a blade judder
across the windscreen, leaving radial streaks.

He repeats the phrase *chatter hop   chatter hop,*

tells me how he shoved a screwdriver
under the window rubber. Broken glass
crazed away easily, over a shoe.

Chatter hop, what damaged wipers do.

OMA

Now her orange Beetle blooms with black rust.
Tyres and seats are tilted. A blade of wing mirror
hangs to the left. It isn't mine to give away
or keep, kneeling in the gutter.
Everything soft in it has rotted.

NAMES

Endpaper, Scissorsmile, Leatherface,
Filetongue, Veinlady, Spiderheart,
Shadowmother, Otherwhichway,
Theonewhotoldmenotto
say again

Greeter, Grider, Grattern, Grusset, Grone,
Grold, Grutter, Gretaphor, Grite,
Gramiscary, Grimmortal, Grash,
Greccessary, Greath,

Greymother, Bloodholder, Winesmile,
Petra Genetrix, History Shell,
Tellus Mater, Heartroot, Woman Book,
Theonewhotoldmewhatto
say again

LUCY'S LIGHT

The rain is slipping them out of their ceremonies
to begin winter, her father walking the garden
threatening to cut down the bare plum
and pear, and her mother running
after, pleading that the trees
will fruit next summer,
grandmother's hurta
eaten together while they ask
the longest moon to scatter silver in
their hair at an angle so narrow that each
sees the bits of blackened iron stuck in grass
at their feet as cloves in the shining flesh of apple.

She is Desperate for Spring

I'd no more ride
that string of rail,
that bronze bracken
of empty carriage
besieging the funfair
closed for winter,
than I'd pass up
May's tour of air.

POSTWAR

Gladys' legs
tanned with sand.
Free spectacles.

Harry Roy
on the Novachord
or Lew Stone
at the Dominion?

Horse casserole.
Bill, tight
as a demob suit.

The curse of having
to act natural.

The Old Battery, Isle of Wight

Recesses once glazed her dangerous candles.
She would kill for one spark.

Now you won't see her powder men tiptoe through barriers in socks,
put on rope-soled sandals and calico garments, buttoned with bone.

Nor will you see her powder, guns, beehive bullets, sailors,
Wrens, matrosses.

Floors, walls, roofs in the cartridge store, artillery, guard room
have been emptied and glossed in black or white.

Her courtyard walls, probed by narrow entries,
are torn off.

The winch attached to her rolling bridge stands wound tight.
But her moat, the sea, still wrecks; saving, foiling.

A Curse on Your Moider

Let the Cassandra dogs be warned off now. Let
every sibilant from your moiderer's mouth be
bleached. Let teeth crowd out your think aloud
with heavy metal crowns that do not fit. Let
each word as it breathes burn you an ice-capped
ulcer. Let syllable-streams wandering miles from
where they start clam up with choke weed to
the throat.

Then may you be taken
by the faces you've talked down
to the place of archives
where appropriate technology be used
to roll the whole Sargasso sea back
through your mind, a silent tsunami.

A Seafront Wake for the Postwar

The ruin on the island keeps away: fragmented steps,
shoulder bone of upper storey arch, lady chapel, rank
of skinned arms cracked at the wrists.

New houses creep near like animals listening to the old—
Teach Me Tonight—magnified through a trumpet
fixed to the mother-board.

My time was blonde scraped up in a froth. Now our white hair
is arranged against purple. From birth, the agenda of regeneration
confuses us. 'Skip it.'

I read future time by Attlee as surely as if those clock hands, beamed
on the wake wall from a light disguised as a camera, are snapping
facts. All of it is skin

though now it shakes loose of flesh, once stock still like rock inside.
An old man's hands flick his horsetail metres.
The wind turbines rush round.

'Pat's been a Samaritan since July.' 'My new man has a boat.'
Sea gatefolds each page of wave and tears.
The Struggle is Over.

Notes

Live Grenade in Sack of Potatoes Story
Nonna (Italian), Oma (Dutch & German), Nain (Welsh) are names for a grandmother.

Once Troublesome
Pocoyo and *Juggling Balls* are both TV programmes for children. 'Pocoyo' is a Spanish word meaning 'little me'.

Mine, Then
Grandmothers often work as unpaid carers of grandchildren whose parents are at work or otherwise occupied. They parent orphaned children full-time. This is particularly useful in communities struggling with the effects of AIDs.

Xylotheque
A xylotheque is a library made of wood.

The Herebefore
Corymbs are stalked flowers, arranged on a main branch in a particular way known beautifully if equally obscurely as an inflorescence. An archangel is a dead-nettle.

The Clockwork Gift
An aye-aye is a lemur from Madagascar, held by some to represent evil.

St Anne's Apocrypha
These poems are very loosely based on the apocryphal stories of Anne, grandmother of Jesus who lived near Jerusalem. Mary, her daughter, was born late in Anne's life. Childlessness had depressed her and her husband Joachim to the point where Joachim went to brood in the desert. Angels told the couple of God's plan to make Anne pregnant and they met at Jerusalem's Golden Gate, a moment captured by countless medieval

painters. Anne became a cult figure in the Christian church, particularly associated with the education of girls.

Turn and Out of It
'Schwa' is the linguist's term for the indistinct or neutral vowel sound, as in 'the' when it is pronounced 'thu'. It is very common in English.

Backpacker
Bastimentos and Bocas are in Panama.

Solar Scientist
I lived for a while opposite a huge electronic advertising billboard. The naked blonde woman advertising a TV programme took hold of my bedroom every night for a long while. I missed her when the ad changed.

Names
These stanzas are made of neologisms, words or phrases I have coined for grandmother, apart from 'tellus mater' in the last stanza which is Latin for 'mother earth'.

The Old Battery, Isle of Wight
A matross is a soldier who assists a gunner. A Wren is a member of the Women's Royal Naval Service.

Curse on Your Moider
To moider is to verbalise endlessly in a complaining fashion without thought of impact on the listener. The word is of Gaelic origin.

Acknowledgements

Thanks are due to Kingston University English Department for giving me a bursary to write this collection. Warmest thanks go to Carrie Etter and Sarah Sceats for their ongoing support and encouragement as well as skilled and perceptive comments which have helped shape this collection. Special thanks also to Siobhan Campbell, Roddy Lumsden and Jane Yeh who read various stages of the manuscript.

Grateful acknowledgement is made to editors of the following publications in which poems, or earlier versions, have appeared or are due to appear:
London Magazine: 'Petra Genetrix'; *London Review of Books*: 'A Seafront Wake for the Postwar', 'Once Troublesome'; *Long Poem*: 'The Herebefore'; *Magma*: 'The Clockwork Gift' (titled 'Rose Coat'), 'Thirteen', 'Xylotheque', 'She is Desperate for Spring', 'Summerhouse', 'Open Plan'; *Mimesis*: 'Sleeping on a Trampoline'; *The North*: 'Fatality' (titled 'The Mechanism'); *Poetry Salzburg Review*: 'The Thike', 'Hoard'; *Poetry Wales*: 'A Curse on Your Moider', 'Experience', 'Shaman Mam-Gu'; *Qarrtsiluni*: 'Lucy's Light'; *Shadowtrain*: 'Unexpected Goal', 'Mrs Campbell of Ballimore', 'Woman, Probably One of the Fates', 'Street Football'; *Shearsman Magazine*: 'Names' (titled 'Say Again'), 'St Anne's Apocrypha'; *Times Literary Supplement*: 'Backpacker', 'Ubi Sunt', 'Room Under the Stairs'; *Warwick Review*: 'The Old Battery, Isle of Wight', 'Live Grenade in Sack of Potatoes Story'.
'Empire' appeared in the anthology, *I Am Twenty People*, edited by Mimi Khalvati and Stephen Knight (Enitharmon 2007). 'Mine, Then' appeared in the anthology, *Only Connect,* edited by Jan Fortune-Wood (Cinnamon Press 2007). 'The Wild Life of Goodbye' is due to appear in the anthology, *In the Telling,* edited by Gail Ashton (Cinnamon Press 2009). 'Experience' was featured as Poetry Daily's poem of the day on 26 August 2008.
A selection of these poems will appear in the anthology, *Identity Parade,* edited by Roddy Lumsden (Bloodaxe Books, 2010).

Printed in the United Kingdom
by Lightning Source UK Ltd.
136318UK00001BA/208-225/P